Copyright © 2011 XAMonline, Inc.
All rights reserved. No part of the material protected by this copyright notice may be reproduced or utilized in any form or by any means, electronic or mechanical, including photocopying, recording or by any information storage and retrievable system, without written permission from the copyright holder.

To obtain permission(s) to use the material from this work for any purpose including workshops or seminars, please submit a written request to:

XAMonline, Inc.
25 First Street, Suite 106
Cambridge, MA 02141
Toll Free: 1-800-509-4128
Email: info@xamonline.com
Web: www.xamonline.com
Fax: 1-617-583-5552

Library of Congress Cataloging-in-Publication Data

Wynne, Sharon A.
  PRAXIS Principles of Learning and Teaching (7-12) 0524 Practice Test 2:
  Teacher Certification / Sharon A. Wynne. -1st ed.
  ISBN: 978-1-60787-132-3
    1. PRAXIS Principles of Learning and Teaching (7-12) 0524 Practice Test 2
    2. Study Guides   3. PRAXIS   4. Teachers' Certification & Licensure
    5. Careers

Disclaimer:
The opinions expressed in this publication are the sole works of XAMonline and were created independently from the National Education Association, Educational Testing Service, or any State Department of Education, National Evaluation Systems or other testing affiliates.

Between the time of publication and printing, state specific standards as well as testing formats and website information may change that is not included in part or in whole within this product. Sample test questions are developed by XAMonline and reflect similar content as on real tests; however, they are not former tests. XAMonline assembles content that aligns with state standards but makes no claims nor guarantees teacher candidates a passing score. Numerical scores are determined by testing companies such as NES or ETS and then are compared with individual state standards. A passing score varies from state to state.

Printed in the United States of America   œ-1
PRAXIS Principles of Learning and Teaching (7-12) 0524 Practice Test 2
ISBN: 978-1-60787-132-3

Praxis Principles of Learning and Teaching (7-12) 0524
Post-Test Sample Questions

STUDENTS AS LEARNERS

1. What is one component of the instructional planning model that must be given careful evaluation? *(Rigorous) (Skill 2.2)*

    A. Students' prior knowledge and skills

    B. The script the teacher will use in instruction

    C. Future lesson plans

    D. Parent participation

2. What are critical elements of instructional process? *(Average) (Skill 2.4)*

    A. Content, goals, teacher needs

    B. Means of getting money to regulate instruction

    C. Content, materials, activities, goals, learner needs

    D. Materials, definitions, assignments

3. Who developed the theory of multiple intelligences? *(Easy) (Skill 2.4)*

    A. Bruner

    B. Gardner

    C. Kagan

    D. Cooper

4. In the past, teaching has been viewed as _____ while in more current society it has been viewed as _____. *(Rigorous) (Skill 2.5)*

    A. isolating, collaborative

    B. collaborative, isolating

    C. supportive, isolating

    D. isolating, Supportive

5. When planning instruction, which of the following is an organizational tool to help ensure you are providing a well-balanced set of objectives?
(Rigorous) (Skill 2.6)

   A. Using a taxonomy to develop objectives

   B. Determining prior knowledge skill levels

   C. Determining readiness levels

   D. Ensuring you meet the needs of diverse learners

6. According to recent studies, what is the estimated number of adolescents that have physical, social, or emotional problems related to the abuse of alcohol?
(Rigorous) (Skill 3.6)

   A. Less that one million

   B. 1–2 million

   C. 2–3 million

   D. More than four million

INSTRUCTION AND ASSESSMENT

7. **Students who are learning English as a second language often require which of the following to process new information?**
   (Rigorous) (Skill 4.3)

   A. Translators

   B. Reading tutors

   C. Instruction in their native language

   D. Additional time and repetitions

8. **If a student has a poor vocabulary, the teacher should recommend that:**
   (Average) (Skill 4.4)

   A. The student read newspapers, magazines, and books on a regular basis

   B. The student enroll in a Latin class

   C. The student writes the words repetitively after looking them up in the dictionary

   D. The student use a thesaurus to locate synonyms and incorporate them into his or her vocabulary

9. **Which of the following is not a technique of prewriting?**
   (Easy) (Skill 4.4)

   A. Clustering

   B. Listing

   C. Brainstorming

   D. Proofreading

10. **Which of the following is an example of a restriction within the affective domain?**
    (Easy) (Skill 5.1)

    A. Unable to think abstractly

    B. Inability to synthesize information

    C. Inability to concentrate

    D. Inability complete physical activities

11. **What is evaluation of the instructional activity based on?**
    (Easy) (Skill 5.1)

    A. Student grades

    B. Teacher evaluation

    C. Student participation

    D. Specified criteria

12. What is an effective way to help a non-English-speaking student succeed in class?
    (Rigorous) (Skill 5.2)

    A. Refer the child to a specialist

    B. Maintain an encouraging, success-oriented atmosphere

    C. Help them assimilate by making them use English exclusively

    D. Help them cope with the content materials you presently use

13. What is a roadblock to second language learning?
    (Rigorous) (Skill 5.2)

    A. Students are forced to speak

    B. Students speak only when ready

    C. Mistakes are considered a part of learning

    D. The focus is on oral communication

14. Which of the following is NOT used in evaluating test items?
    (Rigorous) (Skill 6.1)

    A. Student feedback

    B. Content validity

    C. Reliability

    D. Ineffective coefficient

15. Mr. Ryan has proposed to his classroom that the students may demonstrate understanding of the unit taught in a variety of ways including: taking a test, writing a paper, creating an oral presentation, or building a model or project. Which of the following areas of differentiation has Mr. Ryan demonstrated?
    (Rigorous) (Skill 6.2)

    A. Synthesis

    B. Product

    C. Content

    D. Product

16. Which of the following describes why it is important and necessary for teachers to be able to analyze data on their students?
    (Rigorous) (Skill 6.2)

    A. To provide appropriate instruction

    B. To make instructional decisions

    C. To communicate and determine instructional progress

    D. All of the above

COMMUNICATION TECHNIQUES

17. Reducing off-task time and maximizing the amount of time students spend attending to academic tasks is closely related to which of the following?
    (Rigorous) (Skill 7.1)

    A. Using whole-class instruction only

    B. Business-like behaviors of the teacher

    C. Dealing only with major teaching functions

    D. Giving students a maximum of two minutes to come to order

18. Mrs. Peck wants to justify the use of personalized learning community to her principal. Which of the following reasons should she use?
    (Rigorous) (Skill 7.2)

    A. They build multiculturalism

    B. They provide a supportive environment to address academic and emotional needs

    C. They builds relationships between students which promote lifelong learning

    D. They are proactive in their nature

19. Which of the following could be an example of a situation that could have an effect on a student's learning and academic progress?
    (Average) (Skill 7.2)

    A. Relocation

    B. Abuse

    C. Both of the Above

    D. Neither of the Above

20. Which of the following can be measured utilizing the following types of assessments: direct observation, role playing, context observation, and teacher ratings?
    (Easy) (Skill 7.3)

    A. Social Skills

    B. Reading Skills

    C. Math Skills

    D. Need for specialized instruction

21. **What have recent studies regarding effective teachers concluded?**
(Rigorous) (Skill 7.5)

    A. Effective teachers let students establish rules

    B. Effective teachers establish routines by the sixth week of school

    C. Effective teachers state their own policies and establish consistent class rules and procedures on the first day of class

    D. Effective teachers establish flexible routines

22. **When is utilization of instructional materials most effective?**
(Average) (Skill 8.1)

    A. When the activities are sequenced

    B. When the materials are prepared ahead of time

    C. When the students choose the pages to work on

    D. When the students create the instructional materials

PROFESSION AND COMMUNITY

23. **What should a teacher do when students have not responded well to an instructional activity?** *(Average) (Skill 9.2[k1])*

    A. Reevaluate learner needs

    B. Request administrative help

    C. Continue with the activity another day

    D. Assign homework on the concept

24. **What is an effective way to prepare students for testing?** *(Average) (Skill 9.5)*

    A. Minimize the importance of the test

    B. Orient the students to the test, telling them of the purpose, how the results will be used, and how it is relevant to them

    C. Use the same format for every test are given

    D. Have them construct an outline to study from

Sample Writing Assignment 1

In an essay written for a group of educators, frame your response by identifying a grade level and/or subject area for which you are prepared to teach; then:

- Explain the importance of using a variety of instructional approaches so that all students can learn and master the standards.
- Describe two strategies to meet this goal.
- Explain why the strategies you have chosen would be effective.

Be sure to specify a grade level/subject area in your essay, and frame your ideas so that an educator at your level will be able to understand the basis for your response.

Sample Writing Assignment 2

In an essay written for a group of educators, frame your response by identifying a grade level and/or subject area for which you are prepared to teach; then:

- Explain the importance of helping students learn to be critical learners in the classroom who exert higher-order thinking skills.
- Describe two strategies to meet this goal.
- Explain why the strategies you have chosen would be effective.

Be sure to specify a grade level/subject area in your essay, and frame your ideas so that an educator at your level will be able to understand the basis for your response.

Praxis Principles of Learning and Teaching (7-12) 0524
Post-Test Sample Questions with Rationales

STUDENTS AS LEARNERS

1. **What is one component of the instructional planning model that must be given careful evaluation?**
   (Rigorous) (Skill 2.2)

   A. Students' prior knowledge and skills

   B. The script the teacher will use in instruction

   C. Future lesson plans

   D. Parent participation

   Answer: A. Students' prior knowledge and skills
   The teacher will, of course, have certain expectations regarding where the students will be physically and intellectually when he or she plans for a new class. However, there will be wide variations in the actual classroom. If he or she doesn't make the extra effort to understand where there are deficiencies and where there are strengths in the individual students, the planning will probably miss the mark, at least for some members of the class. This information can be obtained through a review of student records, by observation, and by testing.

2. **What are critical elements of instructional process?**
   (Average) (Skill 2.4)

   A. Content, goals, teacher needs

   B. Means of getting money to regulate instruction

   C. Content, materials, activities, goals, learner needs

   D. Materials, definitions, assignments

Answer: C. Content, materials, activities, goals, learner needs
Goal setting is a vital component of the instructional process. The teacher will, of course, have overall goals for her class, both short term and long term. However, perhaps even more important than that is the setting of goals that take into account the individual learner's needs, background, and stage of development. Making an educational program child-centered involves building on the natural curiosity children bring to school, and asking children what they want to learn. Student-centered classrooms contain not only textbooks, workbooks, and literature but also rely heavily on a variety of audiovisual equipment and computers. There are tape recorders, language masters, filmstrip projectors, and laser disc players to help meet the learning styles of the students. Planning for instructional activities entails identification or selection of the activities the teacher and students will engage in during a period of instruction.

3. **Who developed the theory of multiple intelligences?**
    (Easy) (Skill 2.4)

    A. Bruner

    B. Gardner

    C. Kagan

    D. Cooper

Answer: B. Gardner
Howard Gardner's most famous work is probably *Frames of Mind*, which details seven dimensions of intelligence (visual/spatial intelligence, musical intelligence, verbal intelligence, logical/mathematical intelligence, interpersonal intelligence, intrapersonal intelligence, and bodily/kinesthetic intelligence). Gardner's claim that pencil and paper IQ tests do not capture the full range of human intelligences has garnered much praise within the field of education but has also met criticism, largely from psychometricians. Since the publication of *Frames of Mind*, Gardner has additionally identified the eighth dimension of intelligence, naturalist intelligence, and is still considering a possible ninth, existentialist intelligence.

4. **In the past, teaching has been viewed as _____ while in more current society it has been viewed as _____.**
    (Rigorous) (Skill 2.5)

    A. isolating, collaborative

    B. collaborative, isolating

    C. supportive, isolating

    D. isolating, supportive

Answer: A. isolating, collaborative
In the past, teachers often walked into their own classrooms and closed the door. They were not involved in any form of collaboration and were responsible for only the students within their classrooms. However, in today's more modern schools, teachers work in collaborative teams and are responsible for all of the children in a school setting.

5. **When planning instruction, which of the following is an organizational tool to help ensure you are providing a well-balanced set of objectives?**
   (Rigorous) (Skill 2.6)

   A. Using a taxonomy to develop objectives

   B. Determining prior knowledge skill levels

   C. Determining readiness levels

   D. Ensuring you meet the needs of diverse learners

Answer: A. Using a taxonomy to develop objectives
The use of a taxonomy, such as Bloom's, allows teachers to ensure the students are receiving instruction at a variety of different levels. It is important students are able to demonstrate skills and knowledge at a variety of different levels.

6. **According to recent studies, what is the estimated number of adolescents that have physical, social, or emotional problems related to the abuse of alcohol?**
   (Rigorous) (Skill 3.6)

   A. Less that one million

   B. 1-2 million

   C. 2-3 million

   D. More than four million

Answer: D. More than four million.
Because of the egregious behavioral problems encountered in the teenage world today that have nothing to do with substance abuse but mimic its traits, discrimination is difficult. Predisposing behaviors indicating a tendency toward the use of drugs and alcohol usually are behaviors that suggest low self-esteem. Such might be academic failure, social maladaptation, antisocial behavior, truancy, disrespect, chronic rule breaking, aggression and anger, and depression. The student tending toward the use of drugs and alcohol will exhibit losses in social and academic functional levels that were previously attained. He may begin to experiment with substances.

INSTRUCTION AND ASSESSMENT

7. **Students who are learning English as a second language often require which of the following to process new information?**
   (Rigorous) (Skill 4.3)

    A. Translators

    B. Reading tutors

    C. Instruction in their native language

    D. Additional time and repetitions

Answer: D. Additional time and repetitions
While there are varying thoughts and theories into the most appropriate instruction for ESL students, much ground can be gained by simply providing additional repetitions and time for new concepts. It is important to include visuals and the other senses into every aspect of this instruction.

8. **If a student has a poor vocabulary, the teacher should recommend that:**
   (Average) (Skill 4.4)

    A. The student read newspapers, magazines, and books on a regular basis

    B. The student enroll in a Latin class

    C. The student writes the words repetitively after looking them up in the dictionary

    D. The student use a thesaurus to locate synonyms and incorporate them into his or her vocabulary

Answer: A. The student read newspapers, magazines, and books on a regular basis
It is up to the teacher to help the student choose reading material, but the student must be able to choose where he or she will search for the reading pleasure indispensable for enriching vocabulary.

9. **Which of the following is not a technique of prewriting?**
   (Easy) (Skill 4.4)

   A. Clustering

   B. Listing

   C. Brainstorming

   D. Proofreading

Answer: D. Proofreading
Proofreading cannot be a method of prewriting, since it is done on already written texts only.

10. **Which of the following is an example of a restriction within the affective domain?**
    (Easy) (Skill 5.1)

    A. Unable to think abstractly

    B. Inability to synthesize information

    C. Inability to concentrate

    D. Inability complete physical activities

Answer: C. Inability to concentrate
The affective domain refers to such things as concentration, focus, lack of participation, inability to express themselves, and inconsistent behavior. Areas of the affective domain may affect other domains such as the cognitive or physical.

11. **What is evaluation of the instructional activity based on?**
    (Easy) (Skill 5.1)

    A. Student grades

    B. Teacher evaluation

    C. Student participation

    D. Specified criteria

Answer: D. Specified criteria
The ways that a teacher uses test data is a meaningful aspect of instruction and may increase the motivation level of the students, especially when this information takes the form of feedback to the students. However, in order for a test to be an accurate measurement of student progress, the teacher must know how to plan and construct tests. Perhaps the most important caveat in creating and using tests for classroom purposes is the old adage to "test what you teach." Actually, it is better stated that you should teach what you plan to test. This second phrasing more clearly reflects the need for thorough planning of the entire instructional program. Before you begin instruction, you should have the assessment planned and defined. One common method of matching the test to the instruction is to develop a table of specifications, a two-way grid in which the objectives of instruction are listed on one axis and the content that has been presented is listed on the other axis. Then the individual cells are assigned percentages that reflect the focus and extent of instruction in each area. The final step is to distribute the number of questions to be used on the test among the cells of the table in proportion to the identified percentages.

12. **What is an effective way to help a non-English-speaking student succeed in class?**
    (Rigorous) (Skill 5.2)

    A. Refer the child to a specialist

    B. Maintain an encouraging, success-oriented atmosphere

    C. Help them assimilate by making them use English exclusively

    D. Help them cope with the content materials you presently use

Answer: B. Maintain an encouraging, success-oriented atmosphere
Anyone who is in an environment where his language is not the standard, one feels embarrassed and inferior. The student who is in that situation expects to fail. Encouragement is even more important for these students; they need many opportunities to succeed.

13. **What is a roadblock to second language learning?**
    (Rigorous) (Skill 5.2)

    A. Students are forced to speak

    B. Students speak only when ready

    C. Mistakes are considered a part of learning

    D. The focus is on oral communication

Answer: A. Students are forced to speak
It's embarrassing for anyone who is in a foreign-language environment to be forced to expose his inability to use that language before he is ready. Being flexible with these students until they're ready to try their wings will shorten the time it will take to approach fluency.

14. **Which of the following is NOT used in evaluating test items?**
    (Rigorous) (Skill 6.1)

    A. Student feedback

    B. Content validity

    C. Reliability

    D. Ineffective coefficient

Answer: D Ineffective coefficient
The purpose for testing the students is to determine the extent to which the instructional objectives have been met. Therefore, the test items must be constructed to achieve the desired outcome from the students. Gronlund and Linn advise that effective tests begin with a test plan that includes the instructional objectives and subject matter to be tested, as well as the emphasis each item should have. Having a test plan will result in valid interpretation of student achievement.

15. Mr. Ryan has proposed to his classroom that the students may demonstrate understanding of the unit taught in a variety of ways including: taking a test, writing a paper, creating an oral presentation, or building a model or project. Which of the following areas of differentiation has Mr. Ryan demonstrated?
    (Rigorous) (Skill 6.2)

    A. Synthesis

    B. Product

    C. Content

    D. Product

Answer: B. Product
There are three ways to differentiate instruction: content, process, and product. In the described case, Mr. Ryan has chosen to provide the students with alternate opportunities to produce knowledge; therefore, the product is the area being differentiated.

16. Which of the following describes why it is important and necessary for teachers to be able to analyze data on their students?
    (Rigorous) (Skill 6.2)

    A. To provide appropriate instruction

    B. To make instructional decisions

    C. To communicate and determine instructional progress

    D. All of the above

Answer: D. All of the above
Especially in today's high stakes environment, it is critical teachers have a complete understanding of the process involved in examining student data in order to make instructional decisions, prepare lessons, determine progress, and report progress to stakeholders.

COMMUNICATION TECHNIQUES

17. **Reducing off-task time and maximizing the amount of time students spend attending to academic tasks is closely related to which of the following?** *(Rigorous) (Skill 7.1)*

    A. Using whole-class instruction only

    B. Business-like behaviors of the teacher

    C. Dealing only with major teaching functions

    D. Giving students a maximum of two minutes to come to order

Answer: B. Business-like behaviors of the teacher

The effective teacher continually evaluates his or her own physical/mental/social/emotional well-being with regard to the students in his or her classroom. There is always the tendency to satisfy social and emotional needs through relationships with the students. A good teacher genuinely likes his or her students, and that's a positive thing. However, if students are not convinced that the teacher's purpose for being there is to get a job done, the atmosphere in the classroom becomes difficult to control. This is the job of the teacher. Maintaining a business-like approach in the classroom yields many positive results. It's a little like a benevolent boss.

18. **Mrs. Peck wants to justify the use of personalized learning community to her principal. Which of the following reasons should she use?**
    (Rigorous) (Skill 7.2)

    A. They build multiculturalism

    B. They provide a supportive environment to address academic and emotional needs

    C. They builds relationships between students which promote life long learning

    D. They are proactive in their nature

Answer: B. They provide a supportive environment to address academic and emotional needs
While professional learning communities do all of the choices provided, this question asks for a justification statement. The best justification of those choices provided for implementing a personalized learning community in a classroom is to provide a supportive environment to help address the academic and emotional needs of her students.

19. **Which of the following could be an example of a situation that could have an effect on a student's learning and academic progress?**
    (Average) (Skill 7.2)

    A. Relocation

    B. Abuse

    C. Both of the Above

    D. Neither of the Above

Answer: C. Both of the Above
An unlimited number of situations can affect a student's learning. Teachers need to keep these situations in mind this when teaching. Students are whole people and, just as stress affects us as adults, children experience the same feelings. They usually do not have the same toolbox that adults have to deal with the feelings and may require some additional guidance.

20. **Which of the following can be measured utilizing the following types of assessments: direct observation, role playing, context observation, and teacher ratings?**
(Easy) (Skill 7.3)

    A. Social Skills

    B. Reading Skills

    C. Math Skills

    D. Need for specialized instruction

Answer: A. Social Skills
Social skills can be measured using the listed types of assessments. They can also be measured using sociometric measures including peer nomination, peer rating, and paired comparison.

21. **What have recent studies regarding effective teachers concluded?**
(Rigorous) (Skill 7.5)

    A. Effective teachers let students establish rules

    B. Effective teachers establish routines by the sixth week of school

    C. Effective teachers state their own policies and establish consistent class rules and procedures on the first day of class

    D. Effective teachers establish flexible routines

Answer: C. Effective teachers state their own policies and establish consistent class rules and procedures on the first day of class
The teacher can get ahead of the game by stating clearly on the first day of school in her introductory information for the students exactly what the rules. These should be stated firmly but unemotionally. When one of those rules is broken, he or she can then refer to the rules, rendering enforcement much easier to achieve. It's extremely difficult to achieve goals with students who are out of control. Establishing limits early and consistently enforcing them enhances learning. It is also helpful for the teacher to display prominently the classroom rules. This will serve as a visual reminder of the students' expected behaviors. In a study of classroom management procedures, it was established that the combination of conspicuously displayed rules, frequent verbal references to the rules, and appropriate consequences for appropriate behaviors led to increased levels of on-task behavior.

22. **When is utilization of instructional materials most effective?**
    (Average) (Skill 8.1)

    A. When the activities are sequenced

    B. When the materials are prepared ahead of time

    C. When the students choose the pages to work on

    D. When the students create the instructional materials

Answer: A. When the activities are sequenced
Most assignments will require more than one educational principle. It is helpful to explain to students the proper order in which these principles must be applied to complete the assignment successfully. Subsequently, students should also be informed of the nature of the assignment (i.e., cooperative learning, group project, individual assignment, etc.). This is often done at the start of the assignment.

PROFESSION AND COMMUNITY

23. What should a teacher do when students have not responded well to an instructional activity?
    (Average) (Skill 9.2[k2])

    A. Reevaluate learner needs

    B. Request administrative help

    C. Continue with the activity another day

    D. Assign homework on the concept

Answer: A. Reevaluate learner needs
The value of teacher observations cannot be underestimated. It is through the use of observations that the teacher is able to informally assess the needs of the students during instruction. These observations will drive the lesson and determine the direction that the lesson will take based on student activity and behavior. After a lesson is carefully planned, teacher observation is the single most important component of an instructional presentation. If the teacher observes that a particular student is not on-task, she will change the method of instruction accordingly. She may change from a teacher-directed approach to a more interactive approach. Questioning will increase in order to increase the participation of the students. If appropriate, the teacher will introduce manipulative materials to the lesson. In addition, teachers may switch to a cooperative group activity, thereby removing the responsibility of instruction from the teacher and putting it on the students.

24. **What is an effective way to prepare students for testing?**
    (Average) (Skill 9.5)

    A. Minimize the importance of the test

    B. Orient the students to the test, telling them of the purpose, how the results will be used, and how it is relevant to them

    C. Use the same format for every test are given

    D. Have them construct an outline to study from

Answer: B. Orient the students to the test, telling them of the purpose, how the results will be used, and how it is relevant to them

If a test is to be an accurate measure of achievement, it must test the information, not the format of the test itself. If students know ahead of time what the test will be like, why they are taking it, what the teacher will do with the results, and what it has to do with them, the exercise is more likely to result in a true measure of what they've learned.

Answer Key

1. A
2. C
3. B
4. A
5. A
6. D
7. D
8. A
9. D
10. C
11. D
12. B
13. A
14. D
15. B
16. D
17. B
18. B
19. C
20. A
21. C
22. A
23. A
24. B

Rigor Table

	Easy 21%	Average 25%	Rigorous 54%
Questions	3, 9, 10, 17	2, 8, 16, 19, 20, 24	1, 4, 5, 6, 7, 11, 12, 13, 14, 15, 18

Sample Writing Assignment 1

In an essay written for a group of educators, frame your response by identifying a grade level and/or subject area for which you are prepared to teach; then:

- Explain the importance of using a variety of instructional approaches so that all students can learn and master the standards.
- Describe two strategies to meet this goal.
- Explain why the strategies you have chosen would be effective.

Be sure to specify a grade level/subject area in your essay, and frame your ideas so that an educator at your level will be able to understand the basis for your response.

Sample Response

As a future high school English teacher, I understand the importance of tailoring instruction of difficult concepts to meet the needs of all students. To describe the importance of utilizing various instructional strategies and then to provide examples of useful strategies, I will illustrate with a hypothetical ninth grade language arts class.

When teachers vary instructional strategies, they do many things for their students. First, since we know that all students have different styles of learning, some instructional strategies will not necessarily be as effective for some students. By utilizing a wide range of strategies to teach the same concept, for example, teachers ensure that as many learning styles as possible are satisfied. Let's consider a visual learner in a language arts classroom who only receives instruction orally. The teacher focuses on texts abstractly, and often discussion is utilized. The teacher rarely uses the board and never uses Power Point and never allows students to demonstrate learning in artistic ways. While this visual learner may have the potential to achieve at a higher level, this may not occur as the instruction has missed his or her learning style entirely.

A second reason for varying instructional strategies is based on the concept of constructivism. Constructivism, as a learning theory, suggests that people develop concepts in their minds in highly personalized ways. Take a concept that might be taught in a ninth grade language arts class: hyperbole, a literary term for exaggeration. Strategies for teaching this concept include lecturing, pointing out examples in a text, and allowing students to develop their own examples of hyperbole. Certainly, students may understand hyperbole from lecture alone, yet if they were given the opportunity to experience the concept in those multiple ways, they are sure to have a more complete mental construct of the concepts.

A third reason for varying instructional strategies is based on student engagement. While ninth grade English teachers may enjoy talking about hyperbole, their students may not be so fascinated. By varying instructional strategies, students get opportunities to learn actively and in many different modalities. They experience concepts in different ways and involve themselves in various contexts of the concepts. A classroom with varied instructional strategies is sure to be more interesting to most students than a classroom that relies on lecture or reading alone.

To illustrate how instructional strategies can be varied in a ninth grade language arts class, I will provide an example on research report writing. A research report is a very standard assignment in ninth grade language arts. This assignment teaches students valuable skills in writing and research, including developing thesis statements, analyzing sources, and developing bibliographies.

While a teacher could simply assign a research report and provide lectures on the various methods of designing and carrying out a research report, students would be much more successful if they experience a variety of instructional strategies throughout the unit. I will briefly describe two unique strategies that a teacher might use to promote student learning of the concepts involved in developing and writing a research report.

The first strategy in this unit on research report writing comes at an early stage. As students are settling on topics and looking into books they might use to inform their reports, a teacher might have students conduct a first-hand investigation on their own. For example, a student interested in writing a report on an historical figure might interview a history teacher at the school. Or a student interested in writing about air pollution might conduct a small science experiment by testing the air quality on the side of a highway. While the evidence collected does not have to be extensive, just the act of having students go out into the "field" and gather data helps them learn about the ways in which knowledge is generated. It gives them a deeper understanding about the ways in which the books and articles they will use in the report were developed. This strategy also promotes active, hands-on learning. It gives students who may be troubled about embarking on a large research report project the opportunity to see an aspect of their topic firsthand. It makes the experience more real for them, and it allows them to become more engaged in the process.

A second strategy in this unit comes at the end of the process, as students' rough drafts are written. On the day students come to class with their rough drafts, students would work in groups of no more than four. Each student would have to read his or her paper aloud to the other students in the group. The group members listen and write comments. Then, each group member gets the opportunity to comment on the paper for two to three minutes. After one student's paper is complete, then the group rotates to the next group member. This strategy is beneficial for many reasons. While many classrooms utilize peer review for student writing, by having students read their papers aloud, students experience a performance-type setting to the process, which is more engaging. Also, when students review peers' papers, they often focus on grammar and spelling, rather than more important aspects of clarity, content, and focus.

Utilizing various instructional strategies provides students with richer opportunities to learn concepts. It allows simplistic standards to come alive, and it promotes deep learning. In general, teachers who use various instructional strategies will have more lively, learning-centered classrooms.

Sample Writing Assignment 2

In an essay written for a group of educators, frame your response by identifying a grade level and/or subject area for which you are prepared to teach; then:

- Explain the importance of helping students learn to be critical learners in the classroom who exert higher-order thinking skills.
- Describe two strategies to meet this goal.
- Explain why the strategies you have chosen would be effective.

Be sure to specify a grade level/subject area in your essay, and frame your ideas so that an educator at your level will be able to understand the basis for your response.

Sample Response

I believe that students truly start to become critical thinkers by about the fourth or fifth grades. For that reason, I desire to be a teacher in the upper elementary grades. As such, I have been prepared as a general subjects elementary teacher. My goal in teaching fourth or fifth grade is, above and beyond helping my students master state standards, to help them become conscious of the deeper issues in academic subjects, to appreciate the complexity of academic learning, and to become life-long learners.

The level of knowledge available to us in our society is immense. Knowledge is produced daily, and the number of books, journals, magazines, and websites at our disposal increases every minute. With so much knowledge, it is hard for students to understand how to discern between important and unimportant knowledge, factual and "made-up" information, and useful or irrelevant texts. Messages bombard us constantly, from advertising in places we would likely not expect to opinions that masquerade as news.

To meet those needs, and to assist our students in finding intrinsic motivation to learn, teachers need to be cognizant of the competing demands of information both in school and out of school. They must be aware that students have to make hard choices about the knowledge they receive. Finally, they must realize that sustaining a level of critical awareness about knowledge takes a lot of effort. We don't want our students to hate learning or despise being critical thinkers because it is so hard. Instead, we want them to enjoy the excitement, creativity, and stimulation of sifting through knowledge for the best answer or the most appealing opinion.

To do so, it is extremely important that teachers help their students become highly critical thinkers who use higher-order thinking skills. Attaining this goal in the classroom is not hard, but it does take considerable effort in utilizing effective strategies. One such strategy is in teaching students to develop their own questions about texts. For example, we might start by having students in small team develop comprehension questions (for the purpose of clarification and simple reading skills), as well as analytic questions (for the purpose of interpretation, argumentation, and analysis). First, by having students come up with their own questions, teachers can ensure that students focus on the issues that are most interesting and important to them in the texts they read. Second, by differentiating comprehension from analytic questions, we reinforce to students that there is a distinct difference between re-telling and interpreting. This difference is critical in helping students to understand the complexity of texts, as well as to find enjoyment in the discussion of reading.

Another strategy for encouraging critical thinking skills is to use problem-based learning. Problem-based learning sets up problems for students to solve; through the process of solving problems, students are forced to learn new information in more relevant ways. For example, students can learn about meteorology by studying current weather patterns and predicting the weather for later in the day. The problem is a real one: "What will the weather be like later today?" But the method is focused on relevant learning: Students will be forced to learn about cloud types and wind direction, for example, in order to make predictions. This type of learning is authentic, and it allows for students to create their own questions, be critical of the knowledge they receive, and examine all evidence for the best solutions.

In conclusion, it is critical for teachers to utilize multiple strategies in helping students to become better connoisseurs of information, text, and knowledge. In doing so, we can foster a love of learning, as we demonstrate that learning is not all about correct and incorrect answers, memorization, and tests.

www.ingramcontent.com/pod-product-compliance
Lightning Source LLC
LaVergne TN
LVHW061325060426
835507LV00019B/2303